FIVE STRATEGIC MANAGEMENT ESSENTIALS

Top disciplines to improve leadership skills, management productivity and personnel growth.

EKI OYEGUN- IGHILE, MBA

Disclaimer

All rights reserved. No part of this eBook may be reproduced or transmitted in any form or means, electronic nor mechanical including but not limited to photocopying, recording or by information's storage and retrieval systems without written consent or permission from the author, except quotations used.

Contents

- **Introduction**
- **Innate Self-Analysis**
- **Meeting Management**
- **Conflict Management**
- **Stress Management**
- **Time Management**

Do you know

Your personality

when,

There is No

Pressure?

           PROFESSIONAL SETTING

                    VERSUS

             PERSONAL SETTING

Do you know Your personality when, There is Pressure?

PROFESSIONAL SETTING

VERSUS

PERSONAL SETTING

A swiss Psychoanalyst, psychiatrist and the founder of the school of analytical psychology, Carl Gustav Jung proposed and developed the concepts of personality traits. He developed the extroverted and introverted personality types. This stemmed from his dealings with his own personality struggle. He felt he has different personalities, based on his reactions to different events in his life. His work in recognition, integration and cohesion of personalities has been influential and remain so today.

His theory of personality traits is characterized into

Extraverted (E) vs. Introverted (I),

their preference of one of the two functions of perception:

Sensing (S) vs. Intuition (N),

and their preference of one of the two functions of judging:

Thinking (T) vs. Feeling (F)

INTRODUCTION

Improving the utmost asset of organizations, the human capital and maximizing the most valuable commodity, time, with five essentials. Five essential management skills that will enhance productivity. These skills will improve efficiency, effectiveness and productivity when learned and practiced regularly. There are many areas that inhibit growth and management success within the workplace. Learning to recognize these hurdles and navigate them is critical to success. Integrity and honesty is key for employees and management in working collaboratively.

In this literature, we explore self-analysis and other management aspects that cause misunderstanding and propose alternative solutions. The goal, to improve the quality of employee input and quantity of output with effective leadership. Management and leaders play pivotal role in directing employees to attain efficiency and effectiveness in the workplace. Management and leadership will be used interchangeably in this book because they are often the same in some organizations.

Monday morning at about 8.30am, the rattling sounds of bunch of keys filled the air. Sounds of chairs pulled out, computer chimes as they are turned on, the drawers are opening and closing intermittently. Yes, it is Monday. Everyone is making their way into the office and settling into their cubicle spaces. One could hear the coffee brewing, the sounds the Keurig machine made as it ended cup after cup of coffee. The aroma of freshly brewed coffee filled the air. The fragrance of the coffee was calming. The toaster was in full work mode as well. The aroma of toasted sausage and biscuit, bacon and grilled sandwich filled the air. This was a morning tradition in the office.

The calm begins to set in thirty minutes later. The coffee addicts had their fill. The breakfast club had enjoyed their meal. The overzealous employees were already working. The office was getting quiet, when suddenly, a loud sign from the corner of the room was heard. "Not again!", David shook his head. His calendar alert had popped on his computer screen. It was a reminder that there was a meeting at 9.15am. "Oh, great!" Exclaimed Tracy. Her reminder was on her screen as well. "Yep, I got the call too", said Tony. The remarks filled the room. Monica shook her head, "that room is not big enough, I will just keep real quiet this time around", she said. Michael laughed as he said "Tony, I am going to need you! you need to pull out all your random thoughts and talks from your **comic** bag today. They keep me awake. Thank you". He chuckled. "Yes, please do, I will need some good laugh as well", said Monica. Rodney had been real quiet. Starring at his computer. "My time is too valuable for this hand holding nonsense. Well, what better way to kill time! I have nothing else better doing with my time." Rodney said.

Monica and Tracy had gotten into an argument at the last meeting. Their supervisor never intervened. Monica has made up her mind not to speak at the meetings anymore. This hurts her personal development and growth but it the company is also losing on potential ideas. None of the employees are enthused about the meeting. The likelihood of them listening and actively participating is low. This was a regular Monday morning meeting. They know it will happen every Monday. Yet, every Monday, the mood was this gloom about the meeting. Each one had an issue about the meeting, conflict, stress and time.

Unfortunately, this happens more often than it should. While some managers are aware, others are not. Is there something that can be done to change the perception about meetings? Are there negative impacts to this nonchalant attitude to meetings? These issues clearly must be addressed. One size does not fit all. Managers are not necessarily required to micro manage. However, leaders and managers do need to train, learn and re train on the management of stress, conflict, time and meetings.

Life is stressful, the bulk of our day is usually spent with people with the common goal of earning an income, making a profit or goals. It is essential for each person to learn how to manage the situations that will occur. Leaders and management in organizations need to learn these skills. Employees too should be knowledgeable about these skills. Been aware, will assist them in adjusting accordingly.

Have you ever done a personality assessment test? Why bother, you know yourself, right? Well, the purpose is for you to know and recognize yourself. Usually after these tests, a person can recognize a behavior he/she has always done and categorize it. More importantly, they can adjust when needed. The purpose is really for you to learn about yourself and others and know the appropriate responses. This helps avoid common misunderstandings that can lead to major conflicts. These conflicts will reduce productivity in a workplace or business.

This book will assist leaders, employees and managements become aware of the management skills needed for everyday business. Recognize the signs of weaknesses in the areas and learn how to immediately stop or slow the adverse effect on efficiency. Devise a strategy and a plan to function effectively. Strategic plan is essential to attain any goal. In this literature, you will learn

- 4 key quadrants of people and how it helps in management
- Surprisingly simple techniques to coerce people into increasing efficiency.

- Management skills that are priceless
- As a bonus, you might learn more about yourself in the process!

CHAPTER ONE

INNATE SELF-ANALYSIS

"We are betrayed by what is false within." ~ George Meredith

Many believe people constantly evolve. Truth is most people adapt temporarily to situations. Their true and most dominate side will always surface. It is no wonder so many wind up disappointed. The notion that they have changed another or caused another to change is false. It is important to know the other person you are dealing with professionally or personally. However, do you know who are you? Do you know your personality? Do you know your dominant personality style? Yes, the questions might be perceived as irrelevant but that is the very essence of our many problems. Many times, we assume we know ourselves but would you recognize your personality if you see it? A good exercise is to ask those close to you about you. Maybe you have already tried. What was the result? Aristotle said *"Knowing yourself is the beginning of all wisdom."* Likewise, Ralph Ellison, said *"When I discover who I am, I'll be free."* So many of our problems can be alleviated if we embrace who we truly are. The purpose of self-discovery is not to find weaknesses and strengths only but to learn how to recognize it and adjust it to situations. If you are a leader or in management, how can you control or assist your employees when you do not recognize your traits? Put simply by E.L Konigsburg, *"Before you can be anything, you have to be yourself. That's the hardest thing to find."* It is very important for leaders to learn about their reflections. This will affect how they relate, perceive others and communicate. Organizational cultures are built on their employees. A significant amount of our waking lives is spent at work, so the recognition and adjustment of leaders and employees will lead to greater job satisfactions and increased productivity. Learning about one's self has being made simple by various studies. Hippocrates, Aristotle, Carl Jung and many others are noted four main dimensions of the human personality. A simple quadrant proposed by William Moulton Marston is the use of the DISC model to categorize personalities.

Marston, a physiological psychologist with a Ph.D. from Harvard, in his book, *Emotions of normal people* explained his theory of how normal human emotions lead to behavioral differences. These differences are the cause of most work conflicts, stress and improper time management. Marston theorized that the behavioral expression of emotions could be categorized into four primary types, relating people's perceptions of self in relationship to their situation. These four types were labeled by Marston as Dominance (D), Influence (I), Steadiness (S), and Conscientious (C). Did the responses surprise you about yourself, when you asked about your personality from close friends? Did you accept or resist? William Shakespeare put it best when he said *"To thine own self be true, and it must follow, as the night the day, thou canst not then be false to any man."* It is essential to know and embrace your true self. Think about the responses given. Compare the responses, hopefully you have at least four responses. Is there a common trait amongst all four? This is how people perceive you. We have heard the common saying that "perception is reality". Likewise, supervisors should be instructed to request feedback from their staff. They give feedbacks all the time, it is refreshing and helpful for them to get candid feedback on their performance as a leader.

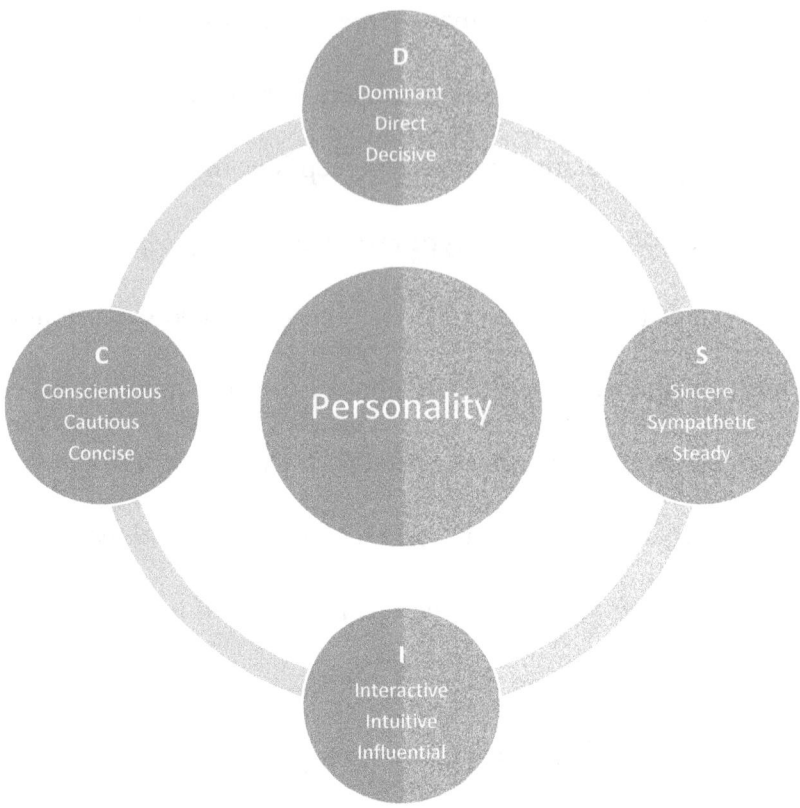

Simply looking at the diagram above, a person can easily select their preferred personality however, there are more in-depth tests that will determine a person's personality. Anyone is capable of being a combination of these personalities depending on the situation. However, the most recurrent and dominant trait is the category you should identify with. The importance of knowing and recognizing your personality is so you adjust. If you have ever attempted to change a person, then you know, it is almost impossible. Learning about you and being able to recognize the other person's personality will help you relate better.

Do you know someone who is always focused on results? They are always quick to act and do not see the need to plan. This is usually a sign of a *D* personality trait. D's take risks, seek challenges and are quick. They can immediately size up a situation and swiftly determine a course of action. They are usually perceived as rude and unfriendly. The truth is they are hard wired to get a challenge and knock it off, move on to the next challenge. Their focus is not on being receptive. They challenge the status quo. They will thrive in positions of control and power. Their doggedness and confidence allow them achieve the most demanding objectives. The quotes below truly capture a Dominant personality:

> *"Be who you are and say what you feel, because those who mind don't matter, and those who matter don't mind."* — **Bernard M. Baruch**

> *"Here's to the crazy ones. The misfits. The rebels. The troublemakers. The round pegs in the square holes. The ones*

who see things differently. They're not fond of rules. And they have no respect for the status quo. You can quote them, disagree with them, glorify or vilify them. About the only thing, you can't do is ignore them. Because they change things. They push humanity forward. And while some may see them as the crazy ones, we see genius. Because the people who are crazy enough to think they can change the world, are the ones who do." — **Rob Siltanen**

Now, think about that loud and talkative person you know. Either in personal or professional setting. Do you notice that this person has an active mind, enjoys interaction with people and seeks constant encouragement? These are the individuals with *I* personality trait. These individuals are highly optimistic. They are born with people skills. It comes naturally to them. Highly inspirational, persuasive and energetic. Their intuitive and creative nature allows them think "outside the box" and produce innovative ideas. Their vivid imaginations create more opportunities for artistic work. They do not get work well within specific details and step by step processes, it inhibits their imaginations. While their exciting and lively personalities can be perceived as a distraction at work, it usually helps build team camaraderie.

The quotes below truly capture the Influence personality:

"You've gotta dance like there's nobody watching,

Love like you'll never be hurt,

Sing like there's nobody listening,

And live like it's heaven on earth."
― ***William W. Purkey***

"Twenty years from now you will be more disappointed by the things that you didn't do than by the ones you did do. So, throw off the bowlines. Sail away from the safe harbor. Catch the trade winds in your sails. Explore. Dream. Discover."
― ***H. Jackson Brown Jr., P.S. I Love You***

Then, we all know the calm and peace loving person. One who always seeks to reduce conflicts they thrive in a harmonious environment. They are practical in nature and prefer to play it safe. They will adhere to historical processes and procedures. Predictable processes that lead to reliable and consistent results is their preference. These are the *S* personality types. They would rather support from the background than lead. These are deeply loyal and steadfast employees.

The quotes below truly capture the Steadiness personality:

> *"So many books, so little time."*
> **— Frank Zappa**

> *Integrity is doing what is right and truthful, and doing as you say you would do."*
> **— Roy T. Bennett**, *the Light in the Heart*

The C personality traits are accuracy, detail oriented, systematic and effective. They often question processes and ideas to ensure thoroughness. They are more logical in thinking and rarely emotional. Their decision and analysis are based on facts and logical reasoning. This results in practical decisions based on rational analysis of obvious predictable information. They prefer to work independently. Even natured and impartial, they are tactful when dealing with others.

The quotes below truly capture the Conscientious personality:

> *"It is better to be hated for what you are than to be loved for what you are not."*
> — **André Gide, Autumn Leaves**

> *"Do you know that one of the great problems of our age is that we are governed by people who care more about feelings than they do about thoughts and ideas."*
> — **Margaret Thatcher**

The reason for learning to understand your personality and that of others, subordinates, coworkers or acquaintances, is to learn to react to situations. This is not about learning about others weaknesses or pointing fingers. It is intended to be an ammunition against mismanagement or disruptive actions. Being able to react appropriately will reduce damage and prevent failure.

Simple steps to applying the *DISC* Style:

- Know your Style
- Recognize the styles others exhibit

- Apply learned knowledge of styles in communication
- Hear the content but listen for the intent
- Know and apply your strengths
- Treat others fairly

Take some time to Practice with the table below. Based on how you categorize others. Write down your initial perception of their actions and how you reacted. Then look at their intent and write down your reaction now. Is there a change in your reactions to the same category? For instance, the person you initially viewed as arrogant and egotistic, do you now see them as just focused and career driven? A person with a dominant personality. Have fun with each category and reflect honestly.

Some common traits and their personality styles below. The table gives a quick snapshot of behaviors to look out for to make a quick calculated guess when you meet a person. Certainly, within an organization or even family setting, a more detailed and in-depth analysis will be required to fully determine a person's personality and all the strengths/weaknesses/traits.

D-Dominant	I-Influence	S-Steadiness	C-Conscientious
Self-confident	Excited	Calm	Consistent
Assertive	Fun	Gentle demeanor	Unemotional
Direct	Build Rapport	Friendly	Sensitive
Blunt	Connections	Sincere	Precision
Opinionated	Comfortable	Unobtrusive manner	Logical

CHAPTER TWO

MEETING MANAGEMENT

The word "meeting" in most organizations today send shivers down some spines. It has gotten an ill reputation. The consensus amongst many, is that meetings are a waste of time. "In a survey reported in *Industry Week,* 2000 managers claimed that at least 30 percent of their time spent in meetings were a waste of time". There are many opinions and reports that back the negative connotation of meetings. However, the fact is that meetings will not go away. They are essential to the growth of any organization. They are part of the human asset within an organization. The problem then is not meetings but the facilitators of the meetings. How then, can an organization change the perception of meetings within their organization? Most employees come with the mindset that the meeting is a waste, hence they are reluctant to engage and participate. This causes loss to the organization. Unique ideas that might grow the organization are lost.

Meetings are a major pain point for leaders and employees alike. The leaders want an effective meeting that generates good ideas. The employees want meetings they perceive as essential and productive. Both the leader and employee have a common aim. They each aim to improve the organization with their skills. An effective meeting is a tool in achieving this common aim. While few organizations can manage well without frequent meetings, many require teamwork and collaboration. Meetings foster real time teamwork, collaboration, brainstorm and information session. An effective meeting sets and achieves set goals.

Human asset is the largest and most effective asset of any company. This is the asset that makes an organizational structure unique. The people that work for any organization, large, medium or small can make or break it. Often, this asset is overlooked because most employers assume they are easily replaceable. Engaging with employees on a regular basis breeds a positive environment. Or does it? Have ever been in an office and you hear the call for a meeting and cringe? Or seen the frown on numerous employees as they approach the meeting space? Why does this happen? Meetings are an essential aspect of the organization. It allows for communication. So why then are employees and some employers apprehensive towards meetings?

Many leaders in organizations are not trained to master meetings. Some leaders simply hold meetings to micromanage their employees. One thing is clear, the intent and content of the meeting must be purposeful. Yes, employees can tell when their management is simply holding redundant meeting sessions just to check off their list.

Now, let us focus on the intent. Managers and leaders need to be honest with themselves when it comes to meetings. Ask simple key questions.

What is the purpose of this meeting?

Can that purpose be fulfilled via email?

Is this directed at all the employees or just one employee?

What would be the impact of this meeting on work output?

When managers and leaders can answer the four simple questions honestly and conclude a meeting is necessary. Their intent is upright and established. Now, they need to work on the content of the meeting. The content will get the employees engaged. Content will keep the leader focused and on course.

To deliver an effective meeting, the leader will need to begin the meeting with a purpose. To help prepare the employees ahead, the purpose should be on the agenda and sent ahead of time to the employees. The goal is to have an effective meeting. Motivate the employees and accomplish set goals.

A leader should arrive on time or even five to ten minutes earlier to the meeting. Usually, most leaders walk in at exactly the time or are a few minutes late. This automatically sends the wrong message to the employees. This is not how to start an effective meeting. The leader does not have to stay inside the office or meeting space, so employees arriving do not feel uneasy.

However, the leader needs to be somewhere in the vicinity, keeping track of time. Walk into the meeting space at exactly the time or a minute earlier, if possible. It sends a powerful message. Immediately employees know you value time and that is commendable. When a leader begins to address his employees, salutation should be the first opening sentence. "Good Morning Everyone, thank you for arriving on time to this meeting". This sentence has accomplished three essential things. Appreciation, Dedication and Recognition. Is there any employee that does not want to be recognized? Or Appreciated?

These simple things are often overlooked. Some leaders do not understand the effect simple gestures have on employees. The next sentence should immediately focus on the purpose of the meeting. A sentence such as "this meeting was set to accomplish (*insert purpose*) goals" or "We are meeting today to discuss how we achieve (*insert purpose*) Objectives". So, within the first five to ten minutes of the meeting, you have communicated your expectation. You have set the foundation for the meeting. You have captivated the audience. Everybody in the room knows the goal, duration and expectation of this meeting. Employees like to know the Why, when and how in any meeting. Accomplishing this in the first five to ten minutes of the meeting will keep them engaged.

The leader of this meeting should have a clear introduction to the purpose. This clarity will make it easy for the employees to focus. While the agenda should already include purpose, time and expectation. Restating it verbally helps reinforce the message. The start time of the meeting is not negotiable. If only half or less than half of the employees are present. Begin the meeting. This is an indication of other issues with the organization. Most employees, if not all should always strive to be on time for meetings. Some, slightly late due to inevitable events. Begin on the set time. Employees present will feel valued and recognized. They do not need to be penalized by waiting for others who are late. Start on time and end on time. If this helps, as a leader, assume that the other employees are not in the office today. Do not repeat the same information already addressed when someone walks in late. The information will be disseminated later. They need to be more punctual.

If you, as a leader get easily distracted by latecomers, then you might consider locking them out. Some offer a grace period of five minutes, and others just one minute before the lock out. Remember the first five to ten minutes of the meetings are crucial. In some organizations, there are policies that support a lock out. For instance, a meeting scheduled for 11:00am, they lock the doors from the inside at 11:05am. Hopefully, this deters employees from being late in the future. Some provide additional penalty for missing the meeting such as a written warning. This is at the discretion of the leader.

As a leader, you should be able to direct questions and discussions to attain the goal of the meeting. Is the meeting to solve a problem, embark on a new mission, change strategy? *You can begin the next sentence with "Today we will be discussing ------ to arrive at a conclusion, decide on the next steps and resolution. The facts are --------. Some information we already gathered are ------. How do we proceed?*

Or if this is not a problem-solving meeting but rather a new mission, You can begin with "We are here to discuss the new ……………. Explore how we can engage in this new system, introduction and conclusion. How do we begin the migration?"

Open and engaging discussion amongst everyone in the meeting will yield more ideas. Encourage everyone to have an input.

Input from everyone will be more productive. Avoid allowing just the eager and usual contributors. The employees less likely to speak up, usually have important suggestions. Seek out ways to get the assertive employees to remain calm. When they dominate the discussion, those that are shy will become more resolute on not speaking. This is not what we want to happen. Leaders do not dominate but facilitate. Get ideas and ask open ended questions that will get the staff talking. Better still, try getting ideas from pairs. Pairing the aggressive employees with non-aggressive might yield a better result.

For some managers and/or leaders delegating roles during a meeting might be the best course. A leader who tends to talk more than 50precent of the meeting time or worse, speaks 99percent of the time with little or no input from the employees, is one that needs to delegate. Delegate one of the assertive employees to lead the discussion. Depending on the size of the meeting, you might need two or more delegates. Delegate another employee as a timekeeper. This time keeper will alert to the end time for each discussion point and inform the leader when it is five to ten minutes to the end of the meeting. This simple act of delegating achieves multiple aims. First, it allows the leader to learn from his employees. Secondly it allows the employee build his confidence and management skills. Thirdly, it promotes ease at the meeting. most employees will feel comfortable speaking or sharing ideas freely to their peers.

While the employee delegated is controlling the discussion, the leader should ensure that It is on track and focused on attaining the set goal. The leader should always interject and get the conversation back on track when employees start digressing. The discussion should not be allowed to wander. At any point this happens, it should not pass five minutes before the leader brings it back to the focal point. I am giving a five-minute lee way because anything sooner might make employees feel confined. This should not be the intent of a leader. A good leader will want the employees to feel free to brainstorm and get creative. Creativity births wonderful ideas. Five minute allows for the delicate balance between feeling constrained and ineffective meeting. So, a leader should be able to meet on time, delegate as needed, keep the discussion on track and end on a timely note. An effective and time efficient meeting would be achieved if the leader adheres to the agenda.

All subjects discussed should be thoroughly analyzed. When a decision is made, and remember, not everyone will agree on this decision, press for closure. Time is important. Impact is crucial. Getting the employees to be impacted and motivated to support the decision is key. The leader should be firm. Repeat the decision, discuss and name the who, what, why and when and move on. When all main topics have been closed, recap the decisions. Summarize, what had been discussed and decided verbally. Look around your employees to get a sense of their understanding. Get your employees to commit verbally to set course of action. Humans are interesting and dynamic in a group setting. When employees agree to embark on the set goals, they become accountable. This could be termed as "peer pressure" or "influence" or even "coercion". People tend to follow through on their commitments when they commit amid their peers. There is incentive to get things done and within time. Everyone serves as an accountability officer to the other. This saves the leader time. Time that would have been spent monitoring, reiterating and controlling progress of task.

Meetings are either useful or wasteful. The intent of a meeting by most leaders, if not all, is to be useful. Meetings are set to attain goals. Meetings are essential to organization's success. Meetings produce leads and ideas. Effective meetings will energize the employees and leaders. As a leader, if you are not enthused and excited about your meeting, then you need to revise. Meetings have a purpose. That purpose and the thought of attaining that purpose should excite a leader. If it does not, then the leader does not have clarity on purpose and will need to re-engage. Have you ever made a purchase because they sales person had so much confidence, enthusiasm and excitement about the product? My hands are up. It happens. Even to the shrewdest spender. Smiles and excitement are contagious. Everyone wants that feel-good product or person. This is what a leader should thrive for when holding meetings. A leader does not necessarily have to smile, laugh or make jokes. He or She just needs to have the excitement in their tone.

Communication skills in leaders is a big aspect that creates added benefit to meetings. Assume, a leader slurring out works as they speak. Shoulders down, face gloomy and not enthused. Reading out an agenda, like it is part of a script. The absence of excitement will make the meeting unproductive. Most employees will not listen. Those that listen will not buy in to the idea. Some might even fall asleep. So, managers or leaders in an organization need to speak with some excitement in their tone. If the manager is unable to, here is a good reason to delegate the meeting to an assertive employee.

Leaders and Managers in most organizations need to be trained on the importance of effective meetings. An effective meeting involves more than notifying employees ahead of time with the agenda. Effective meetings require emotional and rational intelligence. They should be structured and directional. A meeting without direction ends up wasting time. There is nothing tangible accomplished. At the end of an ineffective meeting, both the leader and employees have wasted valuable time. Ahead of an effective and efficient meeting. The meeting facilitator should have a motivating purpose, timed agenda, and deadline. In planning the meeting, the meeting facilitator should get the buy in of the employees by involving them in the planning of the meeting. When employees are included in the planning, they feel heavily vested in the success of the meeting and will contribute. Some simple ways to get employees involved, include sending open ended questions via email to employees. Solicit their thoughts on the issues ahead of time. For instance, "Hello all, I would like your input on _____, please respond to me by close of business tomorrow". This email has a deadline, so employees can act. Most times, when emails come in, employees feel they have more time to respond. Some let the email fall through the crack, because they get busy with other things. Hence the importance of always including a deadline or timeframe for a response on solicitations.

Remember, as a leader, you need to be clear on the type of meeting. Employees need a clear understanding of the meeting purpose. Informational, problem solving, decision making, celebratory, team building or fact finding. Knowing the exact category, a meeting falls under will ease the dissemination and comprehension of information. It will energize, engage and provide value to the employees. Purposefully plan prior to the meeting, properly facilitate and direct the meeting discussions and follow up. Essential steps to a productive and result oriented meeting are:

- *Punctual start time*
- *Vibrant group welcome and address*
- *Exude confidence and excitement*
- *Present clear, concise and focused purpose and agenda*
- *Conduct brief check-ins to keep all focused and engaged*
- *Solicit volunteers or elect individuals for key roles such as note taker, timekeeper and or facilitator.*
- *Review purpose and agenda*
- *Set and discuss ground rules*

Some ground rules that are common in the workplace are: mutual respect for opinions, conflict management, start and end times, respect, interruption and opportunity. These are just mentioning a few, rules vary and can include other expectations.

CHAPTER THREE

CONFLICT MANAGEMENT

The term conflict often implies something negative. Simply writing the word conflict and people immediately put up their defenses. The Merriam- Webster dictionary define conflict as " 1 : fight, battle, war *<an armed conflict>, 2 a* : competitive or opposing action of incompatibles : antagonistic state or action (as of divergent ideas, interests, or persons)*b* : mental struggle resulting from incompatible or opposing needs, drives, wishes, or external or internal demands, *3* : the opposition of persons or forces that gives rise to the dramatic action in a drama or fiction". Reading this definition, it is no wonder, people do their best to avoid conflicts. However, the world would be uneventful and stagnant if there were no conflicts.

Conflicts can grow or destroy an idea, organization and/or relationship. Therefore, recognition and proper management of conflict is essential. Where there is no conflict, there is no growth.

Conflicts occur more frequently in organizations than most will admit. Some are subtle and others are not. Conflicts are an integral part of an organizations existence and growth. One of the human resources departments objective is to hire, train and retain diverse employees. If properly done, these employees should demonstrate varying skills, strengths and weaknesses.

They each have unique personalities, ideas and communication styles. These unique attributes that allow creativity and grow an organization also promote conflict. Usually conflict is due to perception and differences in opinions. A leader should be able to recognize conflict. Some are born with this innate skills, others must learn it. When a leader recognizes conflict, he or she should know how to classify the conflict. Some conflicts require mandatory reconciliation and management, others are discretionary.

Discretionary type conflict should not be totally ignored. It also influences employee morale. If not properly handled, can become a mandatory conflict reconciliation issue. For instance, during a meeting, two employees present two different ideas that are established to be useful by the leader. This is a mandatory conflict that needs to be resolved immediately. The result will have an impact on the goal at hand. A smart leader will work on resolving this conflict on a timely manner. Another instance is a conflict that involves differing opinion on the lunch to be ordered.

Assuming the manager has offered to purchase lunch for the group. The manager has the discretion to select the most popular choice or make his or her choice, over ruling all. This will usually end this sort of conflict. Some employees might continue this conflict after the meeting based on their perception of the result. Some might assume their opinions were over shadowed. Some might use this to destabilize the team. Whatever the decision becomes, if this does not affect the goal and employee morale adversely, then the leader should not make an issue. There is a thin line between being an over bearing, micro managing leader and a good conflict manager.

Are conflicts terrible in the workplace? Not at all. In fact, conflicts breed creativity and growth. However, leaders need to be equipped to strategically manage a conflict when it arises. A leader who has built a team that encourages open discussion and cohesiveness will have less conflicts to tackle. These team members will already know how to tackle conflicts internally and within themselves. Almost any situations that involves two or more persons has the possibility of conflict. A range of reasons are responsible for conflict. It could be due to perception, contradictory goals, philosophical differences to cultural beliefs. Poorly managed conflict can lead to low morale and productivity.

There are several core practices that leaders must learn, practice and train. After the training, a leader should be able to

Recognize Conflict

Accept Conflict

Become the Calming Agent

Analyze the conflict

Resolve the conflict

Manage the result

Leaders need to know that conflict is not always from a malicious intent. They need to view conflict as an opportunity. It provides the chance for an organization to grow in a different track from current. It can provide unique understanding, improved communication and creative growth. Leaders seeking to effectively increase productivity in their organizations should remain calm when conflicts arise. Their position should be to pacify the conflict not fuel it.

This is a fragile aspect since the wrong choice of words or approach can either escalate the conflict so fast that productivity is reduced; or it can decrease the intensity of the problem. Either way, the leader should be the middle person. Listen intently to the parties involved in the conflict. Properly analyze the conflict with probing questions and repeat the answers. Some questions that will help a leader understand the conflict better are:

How did the conflict arise? (Triggers/opinions/prior differences etc.)

Is this a result of malice or differences in opinion?

Is your conflict inevitably or overrated?

Why do your opinions differ?

How can the conflict be resolved?

Sometimes, it helps the employees to review their own agenda's. Asking these questions will allow the employee time for self-assessment. Sometimes, employees are having a bad day, personal or business. They are simply not in the best state. This can trigger unnecessary conflict. This conflict interferes with work time productivity.

Leaders must recognize that conflict is the result of differing interpersonal skills. All parties should be encouraged to list and discuss their reasons for their positions. The true interest and agenda is important. This will allow for a solution that satisfies all parties, more importantly enhances organization's productivity. A balanced plan with open and negotiable points should be explored. Transparency is important in conflicts. Clarify ambiguous positions, so it is not subject to varying interpretations by the parties involved.

Conflict is not all bad. Managers need to learn to recognize loud and subtle conflicts. Employees need to speak up and speak out. If they have a conflict with an employee or management, speak to a trusted leader. There is always a chain of command in most organizations. If an employee is not comfortable with the immediate, go to the next level management. Caution- Employees should always keep the conflict or reason for conflict professional. Stay away from personalizing it or you risk losing credibility.

Conflicts that occur in the presence of management should be immediately addressed. The sooner the resolution, the less impact on productivity. The less impact on employee morale and effectiveness. Management and leaders should not wait but intercede immediately one on one or in the group setting. Subtle conflicts might be missed by management. However, managers and leaders should be trained to recognize it either via snide comments, facial expression or withdrawal. There are many nonverbal cues that can reveal a conflict.

There are various ways to approach conflict. Depending on the form of conflict, a combination of more than one approach might be needed. The five basic approaches to avoid, accommodate, collaborate, negotiate and contend. When you avoid a conflict, the person surprises their own ideas and checks out of the conflict. They succeed in keeping the peace. They lose their idea and the company loses valuable input. This is not a preferred approach conflict. It results in a "lose-lose" situation.

When you accommodate, you are trying to pacify the situation. The goal here is to appease the other party. This is not a favorable thing for the organization as ideas are lost. This can be compared to a "lose-win" case. Accommodation allows for the opportunity to bargain and make a deal. The sort of approach fosters peace and cooperation. Collaboration will integrate all ideas. It is one of the preferred approaches to conflict. This will result in a" win-win" situation. Contend is an approach that leads to "win-lose" situations. The elements of control and domination might not allow for proper conflict management.

CHAPTER FOUR

STRESS MANAGEMENT

Stress is normal. It is a part of our psychological and physical reaction to life's demands. The demands seem never ending. Many studies have shown the increase in stress and its frequency in recent years. The causes of stress vary widely. One thing is constant, our brain's response. The brain is wired to respond when it perceives threat to the body. It signals the release of hormones. This response has been labelled by many as the "Fight-or- Flight" response.

For instance, something as simple as an alarm going off can signal this response. Or something complicated like being hijacked, in a hostage situation or being robbed. These are life occurrences beyond our control. In an organization setting, deadlines, appointments, promotions, demotions and many other instances can also trigger these alarms in the body.

The fact is that in a highly productive work environment, stress and stressful behaviors are effective. Some take delight in stress. The false belief that If you are not stressed, then you are not working hard enough Is believed by many. Have you noticed that employee that needs three to four cups of coffee in the morning, if not more? Or the employee who speaks about not sleeping properly at night because they were thinking about work?

Yes, some employees work better under stress and deadline, however this is not the case for most. What happens to these employees who thrive on stress, when the computer is down with a virus and they cannot work? Or there is mandatory meeting that interrupts their work flow? They will become less productive. Stress management is essential to the success of companies. Most companies as part of their work life balance initiative discuss stress management.

Many experts have shown the increase in stress. The demand for antidepressants are on the rise. Stress related ailments have surged. Stress triggers are different for everyone. To that dedicated employee, it could be the inability to do his or her task at the exact time they need. Stress for a laid-back employee could be increased workload. For working students, the pressure of upcoming tests or examinations could trigger their stress. When individuals are unable to cope, and manage properly, their mental, emotional, physical and spiritual wellbeing, they are stressed. Well, what has this got to do with leaders in an organization? Well, leaders too need to manage their own stress properly so they are efficient at work. Leaders cannot invade personal lives of their employees. They do need to learn how to recognize a stressed employee. Direct this employee to the appropriate resources, If available within the organization. The worst and most severe case of stress, left untreated, is depression or even suicide. Yes, stress kills. This is a very important component of any organizations continued growth. Stress recognition and management can ensure productive and efficient work life balance.

    A leader that recognizes their personal stress is aware. They owe it to their organization to be able to detect, support and address stress. Stress management for a leader is about directing the employee to the appropriate resources, encouraging stress relief habits in the office and promoting work life balance. Many organizations now accommodate their employees to reduce stress and improve lifestyle. Some offer paid break time for employees to take walks, some offer walking or standing work station. When employees seat for 8 hours or more, this certainly leads to added stress.

Physical activity plays a role in reducing the effects of stress. Time is limited after work hours and most are not motivated, hence the paid breaks. Organizations are encouraging their employees to walk more. Some are offering paid gym membership as a benefit. These are smart organizations that have realized the negative effect of stress on their employees. Any form and amount of physical activity will help relieve stress. Think about it, have you been in a heated meeting or argument and hear the words, "take a walk"? or being told to "Go outside and get some air"? these are common ways of allowing the employees "blow off steam"/de-stress. There are a lot of things that can be done to minimize and manage stress.

This should be important to leaders because stress can hinder productivity. For instance, a stressed-out employee can spend an entire work day surfing the net, sulking around the office, day dreaming in meetings or worse putting the wrong data. Imagine a bread factory worker who is stressed and absent minded, mistakenly puts the wrong combination of mixes. This can result in a large batch of useless bread. This is a loss to the company. Not only loss in time but monetary loss, assuming the error is caught before production is complete.

If the error is not caught, then the company reputation, quality and sales might be adversely impacted for a very long time. This can bankrupt a company if not handled correctly. So, the impact of a stressed-out employee has the potential to be very costly. Therefore, managers and leaders all need to be trained on stress management. With the training, they are equipped to notice a stressed employee and act appropriately. In dealing with stress in the workplace, awareness and lifestyle changes are crucial.

In addition to physical activity promotion in the workplace, most organizations promote social engagement time with and between employees. This is a quick and less formal method of reining in stress. Communication, in a social setting with another is very calming. Usually people feel safer communicating and engaging outside the work environment. They feel better understood. they have the flexibility to relate to the employee "perceived as trusted" and not everyone. Communicating your circumstances to a sympathetic ear can be very cathartic. It soothes and calms the nerves.

Here are twelve simple buddy up tips to alleviate stress and build relationships at the office:

1. Engage regularly with a colleague at work (Phone, Instant Message, email, walks)
2. Participate in Charitable causes (Competitions, volunteer, donate time or money)
3. Set time for Friends (Lunch, breakfast or coffee breaks or meeting)
4. Inspire a loved one to check in (phone call, social media, texts)
5. Make time to go to the movies or concert with friends.
6. Reach out to an old coworker and friend
7. Go for a walk with a coworker during lunch time.
8. Schedule a weekly or bi-weekly dinner date
9. Meet new individuals by taking a class or joining a club
10. Enjoy your quiet times (meditate, yoga etc.)
11. Unwind (music, games, dance)
12. Go for confessions or confide in a trusted person.

Engage with trusted friend and family regularly. This is ideal in person but due to conflicting schedules, it is not always possible. However, technology has made facetime possible. While you talk, you can see the person, which is somewhat calming. Confiding in others is not a sign of weakness. On the contrary, it takes strength to be able to discuss sensitive issues with others. If they make you feel like a burden, then refrain and find someone else.

Devoted friends will be complimented that you chose to confide in them. Sometimes, all that is needed to relieve stress are listening ears. And when we say our stresses out loud, somehow it does not seem as bad. Talking about stress issues is therapeutic. Simply pasting the eleven tips in a visible area in the office, might help an employee.

Healthy Stress coping methods

- Go for a walk
- Spend time in nature
- Call a good friend
- Sweat out tension with a workout
- Write in your journal or
- Savor the aroma of a cup of coffee or tea
- Learn a new game/sport
- Work in your garden
- Get a massage
- Read a good book

- blog
- Take soothing baths
- Inhale sweet aroma (scented candles, flowers, fragrance, air freshener etc.)
- Avoid stress triggers
- Sleep, Sleep, Sleep
- Make positive face to face connections
- Listen and/or Dance to music
- Watch a comedy
- Reduce alcohol and sugar intake
- Practice the act of saying NO and have no regrets about it.

Unhealthy Stress coping methods

- Smoking
- Using pills or drugs to relax
- Drinking too much
- Sleeping too much
- Bingeing on junk food
- Procrastinating
- Zoning out for hours looking at your phone or daydreaming.
- Filling up every minute of the day to avoid facing problems
- Withdrawal from people and activities
- Taking out your stress on others (transferred aggression)

Get creative with new ideas that make you feel good! It will alleviate stress and help you recharge.

CHAPTER FIVE

TIME MANAGEMENT

A person cannot touch the same water in a river twice, just like you cannot get time once it is gone. You can make up the effort that will match time lost but you simply cannot get back time lost. Making up the effort creates stress and other adverse effect hence it is important to learn how to manage time. In my opinion, this makes time, the most valuable commodity. Time is constantly moving.

Time waits for no one. When the clock ticks the same time twice in a day, it will either be AM or PM. It will never strike AM twice, well unless the clock is broken. So, we can only expend time or maximize the use of time. Time is limited at the workplace. Inefficient use of time can result in maximum waste and loss. Hence time management is the process of focused planning and control to ensure appropriate allocation that increases productivity.

Unfortunately, in most workplaces and even in personal situations, time is often mismanaged. Time invested wisely is an essential tool to increasing work and personal productivity. Why is it important for leaders to understand time management? Truth is, most leaders already are good with time management, knowingly or unknowingly. That is part of why they became leaders. But it is not enough to be able to manage individual time. A leader should be able to guide and direct the time of his or her subordinates.

Time cannot be stalled, bought or rewound as seen in this literature and many others that have been written. Considering this is a scarce and essential commodity, there is little wonder why it should and does matter to management and leaders. Time can make or break an organization. Effectively managing one's time can increase growth. There are many tools available now that aid in managing time. From scheduling assistant to reminder alerts and calendars. Time can be misused due to distractions, some workplace distractions and others, personal. Some common workplace distractors are range from talkative peers, over staffing, supervisor, unnecessary meetings to changed priorities. While some personal distractors that can hinder work, productivity are stress, medical condition, family emergencies etc. so many things can occupy an employee's mind and make them less productive.

People who focus and manage their time well feel in charge of their life. They are often confident in their ability to perform at optimal levels. They are in control of their time. Organized and committed to scheduled tasks. When people can control their time, they are more confident. This confidence enhances their performance at work and in their personal lives. Some leaders, managers and employees are inborn with the ability to properly manage their time. They simply plan, prepare, plan, and execute.

They are well organized and more in charge of their lives and work. These are people who normally have plan B's readily available to reduce time waste. Their days are based on planned actions not reactions to unplanned activities. So, what is time management? Time management is the effective use of time due to directional planning. Maximizing and making the best use of limited commodity. When time is properly managed, it allows allocated time to set tasks at set times. Time eludes most people. Leaders should not allow time elude them. Time is important to attain maximum productivity at the workplace.

Distractions will occur. Life is not perfect and even the most planned activity can be disrupted. Are you prepared for the disruption? How can you still maintain your time if this occurs? Murphy's Law is that "If there is a worse time for something to go wrong, it will happen then. If anything cannot go wrong, it simply will anyway". Therefore, the skill of time management is important. Time management allows you to plan to succeed, prepare to substitute and plan to continue.

Time management allows continuity in the event of unforeseen circumstances. It minimizes the damage that could have been otherwise catastrophic due to the unforeseen. People need to manage time properly. Organizations need effective time managers to succeed and grow. The good news is that it can be learned. Effective time management is a skill that can be learnt from training, coaching, practice and determination. It is essential in the business environment for success.

The desire and dedication to accomplish goals will determine how efficiently time is managed. So many cheesy expressions such as "time waits for no one", "time is money', "time is precious", "time and tide wait for no man" etc. are commonly used. While these are cheesy, they are true. Time cannot be recovered when it is gone, this makes it a precious commodity. It is moving ahead with or without you.

Most organizations encourage and offer time management courses to their employees. The organizations who are not training their employees on time management are probably not operating at a hundred percent efficiency. When a leader plans their time properly, a disruption in a planned day will only make minor setback.

Your belief and faith in your ability will determine your success as a leader. If you believe you are a late and disorganized manager or leader, then learning time management will not help. A change in mindset is needed. The power of the mind and positive thinking are essential in getting employees and leaders to learn time management. Beliefs have a way of becoming reality. When your mind focuses on the negative, then it attracts negatives. Leaders need to create and embrace a vision of impeccable time management. With their vision, determination, dedication and hard work, they will become effective managers and/or leaders. Once a leader embraces and demonstrates effective time management, the employees emulate. There are several great books, articles, and studies etc. that dedicate time to extensively studying time management. They have documented studies, surveys and result on the benefit of effective time management.

How do you get a leader or an employee to change their mindset? Can Organizations change employee's mindset? Visualize what an effective time manager does. How do they walk, talk, act and work? Are there any similarities with the way you walk, talk, act and work? If you listed everything you admired about their work ethic, can you relate effective time management to them? The likely response is yes! Most of the people with exemplary work ethic are effective time managers. Engage in daily positive self-affirmations. Your inner dialogue should improve your confidence. Internally repeat to yourself that "I am an effective time manager", "I am confident", "I am focused" etc. Repeatedly encourage yourself. You can tap yourself in the back. You should be your greatest supporter. Since your current position does not determine your future role. Always work on these daily affirmations. What would a picture of a highly productive person look like to you? Is this a picture you would like to see in yourself? Make a mental picture of yourself as an individual in control of his or her time.

Changing your mindset to embrace effective time management will increase your growth, personally and professionally. Being honest with yourself about your ability is crucial to changing your mindset. If you know that you are poor with time management, then you have a starting point. Now, that self-realization of limitation is embraced, you are ready to change. If one is unaware or denial about their limitations, they make excuses. One of Murphy's Law says that if a person increases activity time twice as much, then the activity will require double that already inflated time. This occurs when a person is not honest with their ability. It causes a waste in time. For instance, instead of using an hour to complete a task, it ends up costing four hours.

What are some of the values within your organization? If the organization does not promote effective time management then training, education and practice will not have any effect on the employee. It will be a futile attempt. Employees emulate their leadership, their leadership base their actions on company values, ideally. If effective time management is made one of the important aspects of the organization, then the need to learn, retain and practice effective time management is existent.

Why do you work for your organization? Are their core values and mission of interest to you? It is easier to change one's mindset if they feel closely connected to their organization. If the values are closely tied to their personal values, it is easier to change mindset. More important than mastering the ability to manage time, is purpose. If one can relate organizations purpose to their personal purpose then their skill, when learned, will be beneficial to the organizations. If not, they become efficient with time but not beneficial to the organization.

Learning to manage your time effectively will eliminate futile activities but it will also encourage learning. Critical thinking ability is enhanced with effective time management. Daniel Kahneman's book, *Thinking, Fast and Slow,* alludes to the fact that our brain are hard wired to always think and act fast. He describes fast thinking as what we use for our immediate tasks, problems and situations. The quick and instinctive response. At initial glance, this response seems to be the right response. It gives an immediate solution. It saves time, or that is the assumption.

What if, the initial reaction and action is wrong? Let us assume, as loud alarm goes off and everyone in the office quickly makes their way out the door to the elevator or outside. We are wired to flee when we sense danger. We hear that noise and the initial reaction is fleeing. But what happens when we pause and think? It could have been a health alert and someone in the building was in distress. Or it was the fire alarm testing day, which you were informed of last week. Kahneman describes this second thinking as slow thinking.

Applying a more logical and lucid process to decipher the occurrence. Do not just react but thinking before acting. This is not the norm for many and will require mindset shift. This type of thinking can save time. It allows for time to get it right the first time. The wrong reaction or action can lead to a longer time in correction. This is especially important for organizations that require precision. Slow thinking allows you to think about the what, why, and where. What is the aim, why am I doing it? Where will this lead?

Self-Analysis on goals

Self-analysis on skills

Efficiency

Effectiveness

Increased Productivity

Personal and Professional Growth.

Essential skills have been crammed into this literature. These are the basics of the essential business, management and personal skills that will lead to growth. While a more in-depth and thorough practice is needed in each of the section noted here, knowing the basics is a good step. Beyond knowing the basics, daily practice of the knowledge gained here is highly encouraged. Studies show that the average person loses learned knowledge when not used. Johann

Wolfgang von Goethe said it best *"Knowing is not enough; we must apply. Willing is not enough; we must do.*

An essentials workbook to assist practice is included. Learn, apply and grow!

CONCLUSION

Organizations looking to maximize productivity need to focus on their employees. Their front or first line managers and human resources department should be trained conflict, stress, meeting and time management. While all factors are important, learning effective time management will alleviate stress, wasteful meetings and conflict. All these factors of inefficiency are closely correlated. Are the organizational goals motivating? Hopefully they are, if not, then ask yourself, "Am I in the right position/organization?"

Some long-standing tips that have served many in managing their time well are:

- **Get and Stay Organized**

    Make a list, commit the right amount of time on a specific day to each task and you'll be able to check them off. If there is unforeseen item for the day, spend minimum time on it and focus on the listed items. If possible, delegate.

- **Stop Multitasking, Act pragmatically**

To save time, you want to get it right, the first time. Focus on each task one at a time. Allot a reasonable time to each. The likelihood of error will be less. Multitasking, takes more time. Start and complete a task, then move to the next.

- **Discourage Distractors (Minimize controllable distractions)**

Block out time to focus on deadlines. Turn off manageable distractions such as phone, email notifications and alerts. Empower others. When you empower more employee, you get less distractors.

Dedicate break times for social interactions.

- **Plan and Use Break Time**

Avoid burnout and take breaks. It is essential. A break will give you time to recharge and will increase your efficiency with time.

- **Communicate**

Check in with your team. Evaluate your time and the use. What are the items on the list to be accomplished? Sometimes, changing tasks is refreshing and improves time and productivity. For instance, if you are tired of writing and there is task that does not require writing but equally important, doing that, will be refreshing.

- **Allot Bonus Time**

   Always try to add an extra five to ten minutes ahead of time. This can be easy as setting you alarm clock five minutes ahead, setting your watch five minutes past time. Amazing how easy it is to trick the mind to act. This easy trick will allow you make on time meetings or even arrive early.

- **Embrace Technology**

   Technology has advanced tremendously. There are many gadgets that will help keep one on track.

Vacation hours are offered by most organizations because they know the benefit of taking a break. Some organizations will go as far as make it mandatory for an employee to take a specific amount of time off during the year. It is essential for employees to unwind. It will reduce stress. Stress management includes taking time to relax. Imagine how revitalized you feel after a week off work! However, some employees cannot rest when they are out of work. This is a structural problem in the organizations. They are not properly aligned. Any good organization should have functioning backups for emergency situations. While some employees monopolize work, and prefer to be the only subject expert, this is a major flaw for the organizations. All the time expended in training this employee can be lost anytime.

For instance, an employee falls ill or worse passes away, the organizations now must hire, train and play catch up to maintain their optimal performance. An efficient company will always have at least two knowledgeable employees. A smaller organization that cannot afford a two-person team should have detailed work manual and business process. A comprehensive step by step tasks. Standard operating procedure that should be easy for others to follow.

Employees need to understand that their time is valued. Management need to evaluate meeting type and time. For instance, an information sharing meeting should not take more than thirty minutes. Ideally, it should be within fifteen minutes, especially if the information/agenda had been emailed ahead of time. Problem solving, operational, training and other meetings will require longer period but should not exceed an hour. If additional time is need, it can be scheduled later. Management should avoid habitual meetings. This can be accomplished by asking three vital questions. First, what do I want to accomplish? Is there an alternative method of meeting besides in-person? Is there any alternative method of dissemination?

A recurring theme in stress, conflict, time and meeting management is the tracking method applied. There is memory tracking and system tracking methods. Just like most diet systems ask you to write down daily calorie intake to stay on course, so also, we need to write tasks down to stay on track. A missing deadline can cause conflict, stress and result in unnecessary meeting for most. One individuals bad tracking of time can cause a ripple effect. When ideas, thoughts, meetings and tasks are captured with systems there is less chance of loss. Time sensitive work should be captured and consistently monitored with a reminder system, not just a reliance on memory. Calendars, checklist, cheat sheets, memos etc. are great reminders, however technology also makes it very easy now to program all these meetings on one's cellphone.

KNOWLEDGE CHECK

Meeting Management

1) Define an effective meeting in your own words.

2) What is your meeting Objective?

3) List three sample questions to assist in clarifying the objective.

4) Will this meeting be time well spent?

5) Does a meeting need to start on time?

6) Is an agenda necessary?

7) List benefits of Meeting Summary, if any?

8) what undeniably must be covered?

9) what do you need to accomplish at the meeting?

10) who needs to attend the meeting for it to be successful?

11) what order will you cover the topics?

12) how much time will spend on each topic?

13) when will the meeting take place?

14) Where will the meeting convene?

15) Duration?

16) Did you research and validate your information?

17) What roles are the participants to play?

18) Is the style of meeting decided?

19) Is everyone participating?

20) Do you pay attention to nonverbal cues?

21) Do you summarize at the end of every meeting?

22) Do you solicit participants feedback (prior and after)?

Stress Management

The time management quiz will help guide us to the goal of becoming efficient time managers.

A recording key at the end will indicate how far you need to go.

On a scale of 1-4,

l=always; 2=usually; 3=sometimes; 4=never.

How Often do you take vacation during the year?

Do you take a mental health day to unwind during the month?

How often do you socialize with friends?

How often do you socialize with acquaintances?

How often do you take work home?

Do you let work stress linger while at home?

Do you leave work at work?

Do you have a hobby?

Are you passionate about anything new?

Are you physically active?

Do you engage in any sports?

How often do you read a good book?

Do you meditate?

Answer honestly and reflect on how you can change your answers, if needed. Remember stress in unavoidable but we control how we react to stress. It is important to take care of ourselves. Getting physical, mediating, healthy eating and more can help us with stress.

Time Management

One of the greatest factors contributing to stress is our inability to manage time. Conversely, good time management skills allow us to organize our lives and be more productive, both at work and at home. The time management quiz should serve as a guide in the goal of becoming efficient time managers.

On a scale of 1-4, where is 1=always; 2=usually; 3=sometimes; 4=never.

Do you set out time for yourself daily?

Are your deadlines and schedules planned?

Are your objectives documented?

Are you using technology to mind your schedules?

Do you delegate duties?

Are your efforts duplicated?

Are your meetings well planned and organized?

Do you multitask or do one task at a time?

Scoring key: 8 - 16 = Excellent time manager 16 - 24 = Good time manager 25 - 32 = Poor time manager

If you scored above 25, you have lots of work to do to become an effective time manager and avoid the stress that leads to productivity problems.

Try to avoid:

Procrastination, Clutter, Control (total)

Memory storage of schedules, Inflexibility

Do more:

Delegating, Systematic Scheduling

Planning, Prioritizing, Saying No!

Conflict Management

Is there a preferred conflict management style?

What is your preferred conflict resolution method?

Can all conflicts be solved with your preferred method?

Should you always compromise when a conflict arises?

Do you immediately address a conflict when you observe it?

Is eye contact important during conflict resolution?

Remember there are, The avoiding style (Avoidance), The problem-solving style, The bargaining style, The smoothing style. Be Assertive and open to new ideas.

> *Discuss : Assertively but diplomatically state your perspective; Brainstorm possible solutions to the problem.*

Disclaimer

All rights reserved. No part of this eBook may be reproduced or transmitted in any form or means, electronic nor mechanical including but not limited to photocopying, recording or by information's storage and retrieval systems without written consent or permission from the author, except quotations used.

Resource Acknowledgement

1. Merriam-Webster Dictionary
2. Goodreads webpage at https://www.goodreads.com/
3. Marston, Emotions *of normal people*
4. Robert B. Nelson and Peter Economy, *Better Business Meetings* (Burr Ridge, IL: Irwin Inc, 1995)
5. Kahneman, Thinking, *Fast and Slow*
6. A network MCI Conferencing White Paper, *Meetings in America: A study of trends, costs and attitudes toward business travel, teleconferencing, and their impact on productivity* (Greenwich, CT: INFOCOMM, 1998),
7. Eric Matson, "The Seven Sins of Deadly Meetings," in Fast Company, par. 11-13 [online magazine] (1996 [cited 14 April 1999])
8. George David Kieffer, *The Strategy of Meetings* (New York, NY: Simon & Schuster, 1988),

www.ingramcontent.com/pod-product-compliance
Lightning Source LLC
Chambersburg PA
CBHW061444180526
45170CB00004B/1555